Celia Cruz,
Queen of Salsa

Veronica Chambers

illustrated by Julie Maren

Dial Books for Young Readers
New York

In the fabled land of Havana, where rhythm grows, sweet and juicy, like oranges in Florida, there lived a girl.

She looked like a girl and talked like a girl, but everyone who ever met her agreed, she sang like a bird.

When Celia Cruz was a girl growing up in Cuba, she could never hear the magic others claimed was in her voice. When she opened up her mouth to sing, she heard a girl like any other. But when she sang . . .

Her father heard thunder.
Her cousins heard the call of the sea.
Her neighbors heard a hummingbird.

Celia would grow up to be a queen, but she was not born a princess. She grew up in a poor section of town, one of four sisters, though the house was also home to numerous cousins. At times, there were as many as fourteen children in the two-bedroom house! Still, young Celia always stood out amongst the crowd. Her mother liked to tell the story of how a tourist bought Celia's first pair of shoes after hearing the little girl sing.

Like other girls in Havana, she had chores. Some of her friends were charged with sweeping the kitchen. Other girls washed the dinner plates. Celia's job was to sing lullabies to put her younger brothers and sisters to sleep.

At night, her voice carried through the windows, rolling along the cobblestone streets like a wheel or a wish. The people in her neighborhood began to gather outside of her family's front door, begging her father to leave it open. They said, "Her voice is *tan dulce*, sweet like *azúcar*." Her voice, it was said, sent you not only to sleep, but to a nighttime land of angel dreams.

Always shy and more than a little independent, Celia mistook the gathering crowds for busybodies, watching her every move. *"Ay, por favor,"* she pleaded. "If you don't leave, these little ones will never get to sleep!"

Despite her initial shyness, she could not stop singing. In the afternoon, after school, she would listen to the rapid-fire calls and cries of the *pregón*, the street vendors calling out their wares. In time, people would recognize the passion and pulsating cries of the pregón in Celia's unique vocal style.

In high school, she began singing in school shows and local clubs. The music that she loved, el son and la guaracha, blended traditional Afro-Cuban rhythms with the flavor and folklore of the tropics. It was the kind of music that sizzled from the joy of being alive.

Her father loved to watch his little songbird, watch her send a hundred hearts soaring with her melodies. But he was also cautious. "Keep studying, *m'ija*," he told her as she hummed old Cuban love songs while absentmindedly flipping the pages of her school books. "You are so smart. Forget about singing, become a schoolteacher and make our family proud."

Her teachers, however, saw things a different way. "Take a chance," one professor told her. "With your voice, you could earn in a day what it takes me a year to make."

But it is not easy to take a dream planted in your heart and make it grow in the world. Celia was unknown and did not have the kind of connections that easily opened doors.

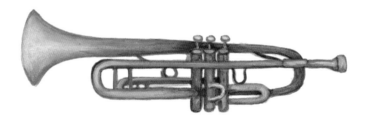

Still, she jumped at every opportunity: talent contests at the national theater and amateur nights on the radio. She never forgot her father's lessons on the importance of education, and after graduating high school, she enrolled in Cuba's National Music Conservatory, where she studied piano, voice, and musical theory.

Then in 1950, she got her big shot. The most popular band of the day was a group called La Sonora Matancera and they were auditioning for a new lead singer. When they heard Celia sing, the way she made each and every note swing, they decided to give the little songbird a job.

At first, La Sonora's public was outraged. Who was this no-name singer fronting their favorite band? The phones at the Havana radio stations rang off the hook with complaints!

At home, Celia began to wonder if she shouldn't take her father's advice and teach school. Was she really the ruin of Cuba's most beloved band?

She stood by the window, looking out at the stars she feared she would never join, and Celia asked herself, "Why do I sing? Is it for fame and fortune and for fans that do not exist?

"No," she told herself. "I sing for my parents, the ancestors, and the saints.

"I sing because when I lift my voice up high, I feel like the first *pájaro* of the day, whistling *buenos días* to anyone who will listen.

"I sing for my little brothers and sisters and the sweet expressions on their faces when they finally fall asleep."

Although Celia was seriously thinking about giving up her dream, her bandmates refused to allow her to quit. As a group, they rewrote the history of Cuban music with new arrangements and a fresh, innovative style.

By the time she left Cuba in 1960, Celia was as beloved throughout the country as the men who made music with her. She'd even earned an affectionate nickname from her thousands of fans. They called the group Café con Leche—coffee with milk—because Celia's skin was very dark and her bandmates were very fair.

In the United States, she became a citizen and her talent was rewarded with a permanent contract at the Hollywood Palladium. But, once she left Cuba, politics dictated that she could never return. She would never again walk the streets of her beloved Havana. She would never again hear the cries of the pregón that were the bass and treble of Cuban street life. It was a heartache she carried her whole life through.

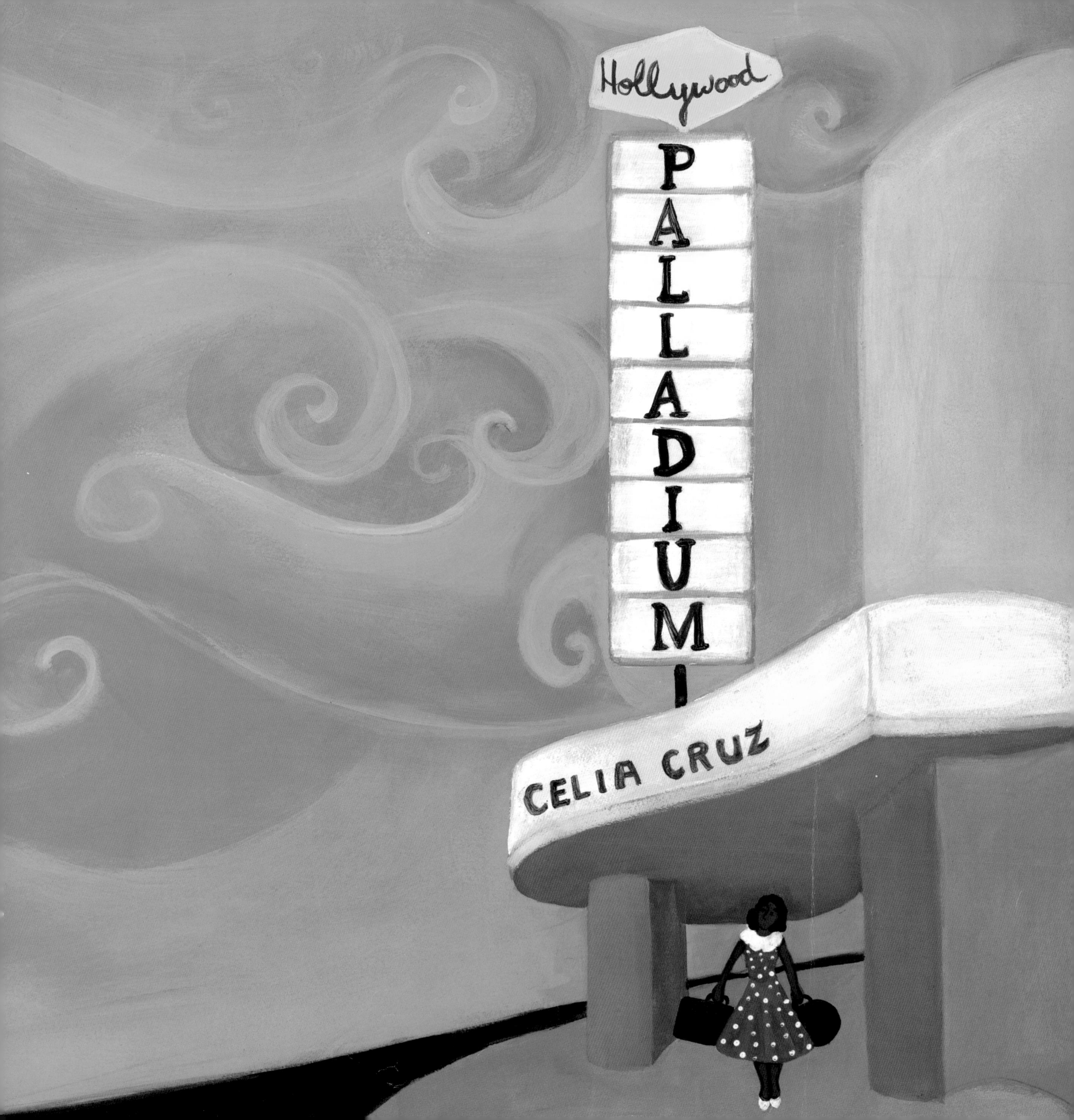
Hollywood
PALLADIUM
CELIA CRUZ

Still, she kept her heart open. Lost loves made room for new loves. And it was there, in Hollywood, that factory town of movies and dreams, that the young princess of salsa music fell in love with a knight in shining armor.

His name was really knight—Pedro Knight. He was the lead trumpet player of the Palladium orchestra, and while he dazzled her with his high notes, he won her love with his understanding. She told him that her heart would always be split in three pieces and only one part would belong to him. One part of her heart belonged to the music and the third piece would always live in Cuba. Celia knew that she had met more than her husband; she had met an angel who would be her companion and protector in this land so far from home.

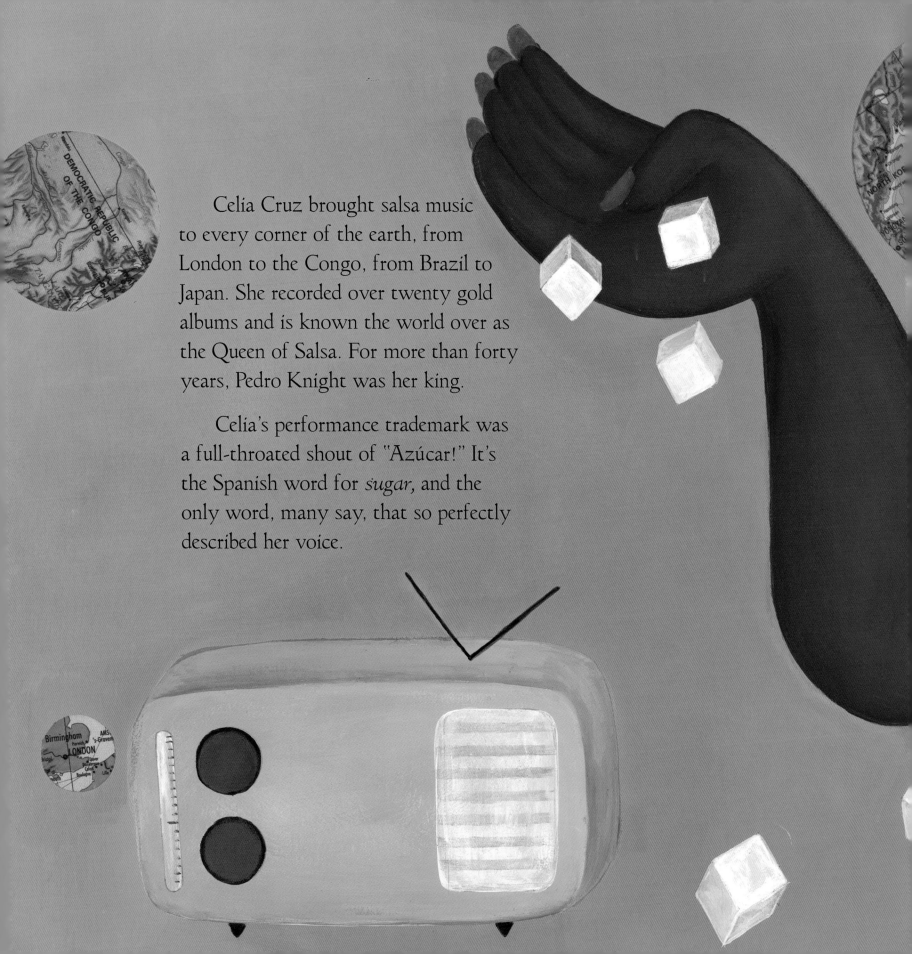

Celia Cruz brought salsa music to every corner of the earth, from London to the Congo, from Brazil to Japan. She recorded over twenty gold albums and is known the world over as the Queen of Salsa. For more than forty years, Pedro Knight was her king.

Celia's performance trademark was a full-throated shout of "Azúcar!" It's the Spanish word for *sugar,* and the only word, many say, that so perfectly described her voice.

In the fabled land of Havana, where rhythm grows, sweet and juicy, like oranges in Florida, there lived a girl. She looked like a girl and talked like a girl . . .

. . . but everyone who ever met her agreed, she sang like a bird.

The bird girl grew into a princess and the princess became a much beloved queen. Her kingdom was music and those who loved her called her not by name, but by the joy she inspired. At concerts, they called out "Azúcar!" and Celia Cruz never failed them. She sung sugar, sweet sugar, wherever she went.

Author's Note

★

I was born in Panama, and as my mother likes to say, she gave me the milk, but the music of
Celia Cruz sweetened it. When I grew up, Celia Cruz became a role model for me because she was
Latinegra. She taught me that despite the common media images, Latinas come in all colors. As a
journalist at *Newsweek*, I had the opportunity to interview Ms. Cruz for a cover story about Latin
music. Honestly, it wasn't my best interview. I was too in awe to ask many questions. Instead, I sat
and listened, soaking in her beauty, her grace, the amazing rhythms of the voice that I'd heard so
many times on records and CDs.

Celia Cruz was born on October 21 in the Santo Suárez area of Havana, Cuba. When she was
fourteen years old, Celia Cruz began singing in local talent shows. A classically trained musician who
helped give life and spirit to Latin American dance music, she studied music theory, piano, and voice
at Cuba's National Music Conservatory. She joined La Sonora Matancera in 1950 and along with that
group recorded the songs that would become classics of Afro-Cuban music. These songs include
"Yembe Laroco," "Burundanga," and "Caramelo." By the end of that decade, the popularity of the
group propelled Celia to international fame. On July 15, 1960, she left Cuba and moved to the United
States. In 1961, she became an American citizen, though she dreamed her entire life of returning to
Cuba and visiting her mother's grave.

While Celia Cruz would eventually become known as the Queen of Salsa, she was a songstress
who thrived on collaboration. Together with orchestra leader Tito Puente, she helped to ignite the
"salsa boom" of the 1970s. But that was only the beginning of the way in which Celia Cruz would
begin her passionate, joyful work as an ambassador of Afro-Cuban music. Her musical pairings
transcended race, generation, and nationality. The artists she collaborated with ranged from salseros

such as the Fania All-Stars, Willie Colón, Gloria Estefan, and Ray Barretto, to R&B legends Aretha Franklin and Patti LaBelle, to world music doyenne David Byrne, to Haitian-American hip-hop producer Wyclef Jean. She taught me, she taught the world, that salsa was more than music for Latinos; in it was contained *la esencia de la vida*, the joy, the pain, the bone and marrow, the very essence of life to which all people around the world could connect.

In her life, Celia Cruz recorded more than seventy albums, many of which went gold or platinum. She won five Grammy Awards and appeared in ten movies, including the critically acclaimed *Mambo Kings*. In Africa, she performed at the sold-out concert that was the prelude to the famous "Rumble in the Jungle" boxing match between Muhammad Ali and Joe Frazier. She received a star on the Hollywood Walk of Fame. October 25 was declared "Celia Cruz Day" in San Francisco. In Miami, a street is named Celia Cruz Way. On July 16, 2003, Celia Cruz passed away, and music lovers the world over mourned her death. She more than witnessed history, she transformed it: from a revolution in Cuba to a revolution in Latin music.

As a girl, princess stories were my favorite—Sleeping Beauty, Snow White, Cinderella. But I never read a story about a princess who looked like me. I wrote *Celia Cruz, Queen of Salsa* because I wanted to write about this incredible woman who became music royalty. Yes, this is a story of a great beauty who enjoyed a great romance, but it is also about a woman who became a queen because of her talent, her hard work, her creativity, and her spirit. Celia Cruz was still alive when I first wrote this book, but I hope that its publication is a worthy tribute to her memory. For me, her music and her life is a reminder of the sweetest things in life.

Azúcar!

★

Glossary

ay!   an expression of surprise, like "Hey" or "Oh!"

azúcar   sugar

dulce   sweet

Latinegra   slang for a black Latina, a Latina with dark skin.

m'ija   a term of affection for a girl or young woman, a contraction of *mi hija,* which means "my daughter."

pájaro   bird

por favor   please

pregón   the official translation is "proclamation," as in a town crier, proclaiming the latest news. It is also Cuban slang for a street vendor.

salsa   the official translation is "sauce," but here it is referring to a style of Afro-Cuban-based dance music, popular in Latin America. Celia was instrumental in the creation of salsa when she came to the U.S. in the 1960s and meshed her talent with other musicians and bandleaders to create the new music called salsa—among the musicians were Tito Puente, Johnny Pacheco, and Willie Colón.

☆ ☆

Selected Discography

With over seventy albums to choose from, it is hard to select just a few of Celia Cruz's albums. Here are ten from the most distinct periods in her career:

★ **Homenaje a Los Santos**
An early collection of sacred music

★ **Canciones Premiades de Celia Cruz**
A great example of her early work with the Sonora Matancera

★ **Celia and Johnny**
The first of her collaborations with the legendary bandleader Johnny Pacheco

★ **Live at Yankee Stadium, Volume 1 and 2**
Celia's debut with the Fania All-Stars. Listen for the magnetic effect of a stadium full of fans, calling out the chorus "colora" on "Bemba Colora," one of Celia's 1960s hits.

★ **Ritmo en el Corazón**
Her Grammy Award–winning collaboration with Ray Barretto

★ **Celia's Duets**
The best of twenty years of collaborations with Celia's favorites, including Willie Colón, Caetano Veloso, Los Fabulosos Cadillacs

★ **Mi Vida Es Cantar**
A popular 1990s album. "La Vida Es Carnaval" was an international dance club hit.

★ **Celia Cruz and Friends; A Night of Salsa**
More of Celia with the artists she loved to play with—Tito Puente, Johnny Pacheco, and the up-and-coming salsa singer La India

★ **La Negra Tiene Tumbao**
Winner of a 2002 Latin Grammy and a 2003 Grammy.

★ **Regalo del Alma (Gift from the Soul)**
Celia's last album, recorded when she was already suffering the effects of the brain tumor that would take her life. Almost prophetic in its sweetness, the final gift from Celia to the world.

★

Por mis sobrinas, Magdalena y Sophia
—VC

To my beautiful grandma Maren, who has always inspired me to follow my heart and embrace life to its fullest
—JM

★

DIAL BOOKS FOR YOUNG READERS
★
A division of Penguin Young Readers Group
Published by The Penguin Group
Penguin Group (USA) Inc., 375 Hudson Street, New York, NY 10014, U.S.A.
Penguin Group (Canada), 10 Alcorn Avenue, Toronto, Ontario, Canada M4V 3B2 (a division of Pearson Penguin Canada Inc.)
Penguin Books Ltd, 80 Strand, London WC2R 0RL, England
Penguin Ireland, 25 St. Stephen's Green, Dublin 2, Ireland (a division of Penguin Books Ltd)
Penguin Group (Australia), 250 Camberwell Road, Camberwell, Victoria 3124, Australia (a division of Pearson Australia Group Pty Ltd)
Penguin Books India Pvt Ltd, 11 Community Centre, Panchsheel Park, New Delhi - 110 017, India
Penguin Group (NZ), Cnr Airborne and Rosedale Roads, Albany, Auckland 1310, New Zealand (a division of Pearson New Zealand Ltd)
Penguin Books (South Africa) (Pty) Ltd, 24 Sturdee Avenue, Rosebank, Johannesburg 2196, South Africa
Penguin Books Ltd, Registered Offices: 80 Strand, London WC2R 0RL, England
★
Text copyright © 2005 by Veronica Chambers ★ Illustrations copyright © 2005 by Julie Maren ★ All rights reserved.
Designed by Peonia Vázquez-D'Amico ★ Text set in ItalianAElectric ★ The illustrations were done in acrylic and collage on bristol board.
★
Library of Congress Cataloging-in-Publication Data
Chambers, Veronica.
Celia Cruz, queen of salsa / Veronica Chambers ; illustrated by Julie Maren.
p. cm.
ISBN 978-0-8037-2970-4
1. Cruz, Celia—Juvenile literature. 2. Singers—Latin America—Biography—Juvenile literature.
I. Maren, Julie, date. II. Title.
ML3930.C96C43 2005
782.42164'092—dc22
2004018960
★
Manufactured in China on acid-free paper ★ 10 9 8 7 6 5 4 3
★

In honor of Celia Cruz, Veronica Chambers and her husband, Jason Clampet have established the Celia Cruz scholarship in music at Simon's Rock College, Veronica's alma mater. A percentage of all royalties from this book shall go to further build the endowment of this scholarship. Tax deductible donations can be sent to:

Simon's Rock College
Development Office
84 Alford Road
Great Barrington, MA 01230

Please note in the memo section of your check that the donation is for the Celia Cruz scholarship in music. Muchísimas gracias!